50 THINGS TO KNOW
BOOK SERIES
REVIEWS FROM READERS

I recently downloaded a couple of books from this series to read over the weekend thinking I would read just one or two. However, I so loved the books that I read all the six books I had downloaded in one go and ended up downloading a few more today. Written by different authors, the books offer practical advice on how you can perform or achieve certain goals in life, which in this case is how to have a better life.

The information is simple to digest and learn from, and is incredibly useful. There are also resources listed at the end of the book that you can use to get more information.

50 Things To Know To Have A Better Life: Self-Improvement Made Easy!

Author Dannii Cohen

This book is very helpful and provides simple tips on how to improve your everyday life. I found it to be useful in improving my overall attitude.

50 Things to Know For Your Mindfulness & Meditation Journey
Author Nina Edmondso

Quick read with 50 short and easy tips for what to think about before starting to homeschool.

50 Things to Know About Getting Started with Homeschool by Author Amanda Walton

I really enjoyed the voice of the narrator, she speaks in a soothing tone. The book is a really great reminder of things we might have known we could do during stressful times, but forgot over the years.

Author Harmony Hawaii

There is so much waste in our society today. Everyone should be forced to read this book. I know I am passing it on to my family.

50 Things to Know to Downsize Your Life: How To Downsize, Organize, And Get Back to Basics

Author Lisa Rusczyk Ed. D.

Great book to get you motivated and understand why you may be losing motivation. Great for that person who wants to start getting healthy, or just for you when you need motivation while having an established workout routine.

50 Things To Know To Stick With A Workout: Motivational Tips To Start The New You Today

Author Sarah Hughes

50 THINGS TO KNOW ABOUT LEADERSHIP

Celebrities on leadership

RYAN JARVIS CORNELIUS

Cover designed by: Ivana Stamenkovic
Cover Image: https://pixabay.com/photos/businessman-tie-
blue-suit-banner-4785283/

CZYK Publishing Since 2011.

50 Things to Know

Lock Haven, PA
All rights reserved.
ISBN: 9798698150237

50 THINGS TO KNOW ABOUT LEADERSHIP

BOOK DESCRIPTION

Do you know why you have enemies? Do you applaud yourself when you fall? Do you consider yourself, fearless? If you answered yes, then this book is for you.

Leadership Tips by Ryan Jarvis Cornelius informs readers that leadership is in everyone and is everywhere.

On each page, one word will show you see those qualities.

By the time you finish this book, you will look at people in a different light.

TABLE OF CONTENTS

18. Wisdom
19. Lifestyle
20. Grow
21. Dignity
22. Integrity
23. Resilience
24. Fearless
25. Character
26. Encourage
27. Maximum
28. Unfollows
29. System
30. Peace of Mind
31. Motivated
32. Inspire
33. Order
34. Truth
35. Time
36. Overcome
37. Unashamed
38. Good Guys
39. Role Models
40. Hope
41. Chaos
42. Stand
43. Honesty

DEDICATION

I dedicate this book to my mom Viona Cornelius.

ABOUT THE AUTHOR

Leadership has always been in my life, but I never took it seriously until now. I am not employed and have not been for about five years now. Considerable expenses I was unable to pay like I usually do. Additionally, I am in a new town. I grew up in Hollywood, FL. Now I am living in Atlanta, GA. Growing up, building a lot of character within me to deal with the conditions I am in now. That character also helped me to be the leader I am now. I had two life-saving surgeries. One was when I was a teen, and the other, I was in my early 30's. In addition to the surgeries, I battled seizures and took meds for some time. I have suffered financial difficulties that disabled me from going to school numerous times. Those same difficulties disabled me from going to the dentist and the doctor—all of this in 37 years. I would not say I am homeless, but I am close. I have been pretty close to it for a while. Thankful for GOD, my family, and friends for not allowing it to get that far. I just took care of myself the best way that I could.

I have no clue where I will be if I did not write to express myself. I write poetry, articles, screenplays, and business letters. I love storytelling. Reading and watching YouTube videos helps me to learn still. To me, it is all therapeutic. Besides, it helps me keep my mind off of what's going on around me. I often use my iPhone 7 to do everything due to the circumstances around me. I may not have phone service, but there is WIFI everywhere. It's much more complicated, but leaders do not make excuses. There are too many ways to get things done, and, in my position, I cannot turn too much away. I am local Since I do not have the funds to travel. If I did, I would love to.

You could find me on Facebook, Instagram, and Twitter

Facebook:
https://www.facebook.com/profile.php?id=10005502
1724144

Instagram; https://www.instagram.com/rjc33020954/

Twitter: https://mobile.twitter.com/rjc33020

Leadership I look anywhere to find. As I mentioned, it is a lifestyle for me and all of us. I drove up to Atlanta, GA, and in three months, I was in an accident. Matters became worse when I found out it was unrepairable. The vehicle was brand new. I was upset for like 15 minutes. Within a week, I had a new one, but I have no GA license. So, I had to park it. I worked as an independent contractor delivering food. In the midst, I was building my business. I developed a page on my old Facebook account called Encouraging Cards. I call it old since I no longer have access to it.

Hackers changed my email, so I cannot reset it. I used the same email to sign up for an Instagram account. The same happened to that one. I lost access to all of the pictures for the business pages I had on both versions. I created a logo a few years ago for encouraging cards. On it at first, I posted scriptures. Then I used celebrity quotes. When I applied to write 50 things about leadership, I was excited. I was more excited I was offered the opportunity. I felt it was an easy opportunity for me. I already put together the material I already had. I use celebrities and icons. There are public figures and could be very impactful in ensuring that people know that leadership is everywhere. We are all leaders. Not all of us lead correctly, but it is there. What I do is I filter out the bad. I look at people I do not like or despise and find something that I could use as a leader. Take drug lords as an example. I hate that they kill their people and sell drugs each day. I grew up seeing that, but one late night I thought about their business minds. I thought about how they do not make or use excuses, and I used the same method to lead. If I see someone could have the zeal and passion for doing wrong, I could have the same to do right. Leading is the right thing to do in life. It's suitable for anyone—one of the main reasons for me to be involved in this. Someone inspired me, and I want to inspire someone else.

1. LEADERS

Martin Luther King Jr

*"The time is always right to do
what's right."*

Right now, he's known for being a crucial part of
black history, but as I studied him, I saw much more.
Martin was a leader out of the womb. When I was
young, I did not see it that way, since I am studying
leadership, it's not hard to see. He was the second of
three children raised in Atlanta, GA. His mom
appointed him Michael at his birth. Shortly after, they
changed to Martin. From birth, he was always around
religious folk. Martin grew up in a religious family.
Like any other kid, Martin was active. When his
father gave him "whippings," Martin just stood there.
I was not born when he was here but knew that it was
something about him. So first, I looked up his name.
The name Martin means warrior. He saw his father
stand against segregation and discrimination. His
family had him singing hymns in the church, reciting
bible verses, and attending church events. By the time
he aged, he was ready to put it all into action. The

qualities of a leader were always there for him. Unfortunately, he left us, but he said he will not be here to see the significant changes we see now. His memorable" I have a dream speech" still echoes across the United States. King has been resting in peace since 1968. No, he wasn't perfect, but who is? He strived to live his life in peace and wanted others to do the same. Leadership was in him before birth. This next celebrity will describe Envy and how it is dealt with when it comes to leadership.

2. ENEMIES

Marshall Bruce Mathers 3rd

"We will always have enemies."

Many know him best as a rapper—one of the best in history. Marshall was born in Missouri. His parents were musicians, but he was not raised by them both. His mom Debbie decided to raise their only son alone after his father's departure. Marshall lived in homes around Missouri and Michigan. Marshall was a happy and quiet kid growing up in a middle-class neighborhood. He was beaten up much for being the only white boy with a family in the area. Even as a kid, he was a leader that did not understand why he had enemies. He became highly interested in storytelling. Shortly after, he discovered hip hop. It wasn't long before he converted to it. His stepdad began to mentor him. Things were going well, but a tragic event changed everything. An event that left him very discouraged. He felt it was all his fault. The discouragement made him contemplate quitting. He occurred to be considering no longer pursue a career in hip hop. To add the pain, his relationship with his mom started getting rocky. His troubles continued as he aged yet, he stood firm. He resurrected what he thought he killed. He began to pursue a career in hip hop. Since he wanted to establish himself as a rapper, he needed a stage name. A unique stage name" Eminem," he adopted and saw much success on and off the stage. Despite it, he was often facing legal issues. He found why he had enemies after all of these years. Leaders have enemies. Many former and current stars say that. Leadership is an aspect that we all possess. He is one of the most historic musicians we have ever seen. He may not have handled it right, but we do have enemies. He had enemies since he often dealt with leadership. My next celebrity will explain why leaders are hated and why it fuels us.

3. LEARN

Missy Elliot

"Give People The Obligation

To Learn From Their Mistakes" She was born in Virginia. Her gift for music was evident during her childhood. At four years old, what her family saw did not shock them. They noticed her perform. Once she got older, she was active in the church choir. Her love for music was evident, but it didn't hide her other talents. She was smart in school and a class clown. Multitalented, but she felt that no one would take her seriously. There was comfort in her being the class clown. According to her, it helped her develop bonds quickly. Since she was highly advanced, she was ahead of her class. Despite it, the issues she faced at home were getting worse. Those difficulties in her neighborhood and household fueled her to make it to where she did. She practically perfected her music. I am not saying she is not great, but leaders understand that there is always room to be better. Everything she put her hands on in the early 1990s was prosperous. She collaborated with a childhood friend, and the hits just kept coming. Sadly, it could not cover what she was dealing with on the inside of her. In 2008, Elliot was diagnosed with "graves' disease." The disease affected her body and life. Her weight was dropping, and her eyes were bulging. Her blood pressure was always up just by overworking her body. Another artist that she worked with noticed she was complaining about headaches and that rest of her symptoms. Soon after, she chose to step away from the industry. She ate correctly, exercised, and take the medication she needed, so this disease is under control. Her most recent picture in 2018 proves that she has it under control. Elliot looks amazing. Now Elliot is back on the music scene. She even started producing on a small screen. Maybe she will appear on the big screen as well. Storms did rage in her life rage, but her mind stayed on the beauty.

4. FOCUSED

Louisa May Alcott

*"I am not afraid of storms for I
am learning how to sail the ship."*

Louise was born on November 29, 1832. Her
birthplace is Philadelphia, Pennsylvania. She was
born in a town that was called Germantown. Alcott
was one of four daughters born to Amos Alcott and
Abby May. As a child, she was a tomboy, lived in
numerous places, and saw her family struggles.
Maybe they helped her find her purpose. As she aged,
the battles did. Due to those recurring issues, she
worked hard to help support them. Writing helped
them and helped her escape from the troubles. In the
early 1860s, she found critical success in what she
loved. The late naturalist inspired her to go on. I
think it was already there. The naturalist just
resurrected it. Between him and her father, she was
well-educated. Her father was pretty strict on her due
to her tomboyish behavior. Early in her career, she
used pen names to write short stories and novels for
adults. Alcott wrote books, and her focus was mostly

on passion and revenge. In 1868, she published Little Women. That story focused on where she grew up. The moral to her life story is pretty simple. She saw the beauty in their storms. When she got old enough, it was more evident. You have to see the beauty in the things you go through. There is always something that will come out of it. Many of us leaders do not overreact when bad things come our way. We tend to remain focused. She saw her family problems and did what she needed to solve them.

5. SOLVERS

General Colin Powell

"Leadership is Solving Problem."

His life began in Harlem, NY. He has earned the right to be called one of those figures is one of the most outstanding soldiers in U.S. history Colin Powell. Powell was born in 1937. His childhood began in South Bronx. There he attended Morris High School. In 1954, he graduated. Most of his time during school, he worked at a local baby furniture store. While there, he inherited many skills, and one of them was problem-solving. He often helped local families on the sabbath. Powell took pride in being a great Samaritan during his teenage and college years. In 1958, he obtained a Bachelor of Science degree in Geology from the city college not too far from his hometown and an MBA from George Washington University in 1971. By this point, being a problem solver was evident. He enrolled to be a professional soldier of 35 years. Now, he holds a variety of command and staff positions. At 83 years of age, he has a memorable, honorable resume. As you could see, he spent his career living that quote. The mindset to solve was always there, and truthfully, it should be. Solving problems is more than a desire; it's a lifestyle. There is a better way to leave this world knowing that you spent much time trying to make it better by solving problems. So, when his time comes, there will be smiles just as well as tears.

6. SACRIFICE

Heath Ledger

*"Sacrifice comes before Success
even in the Dictionary."*

Ledger quoted this in one of my favorite films
(The Dark Night). He was the joker. Ledger was
born in Australia. Wealth was not an issue for him.
Engineering was a part of his family lineage, but he
desired to be a leader on-screen. His older sister gave
him some pointers to do. She was an actress herself.
After studying to perfect the craft of acting, he and
Kate noticed that playing that leading role on screen
was in him all along. Those events he faced as a child
led him to drama. Throughout his time in school,
heath was acting. So enthusiastic until he left school
to pursue a career into it. Ledger had a rather busy
career in Australia. Over there, he was recognized as
a popular actor by producers in the United States.
When he came to the U.S. himself, he portrayed a
variety of roles. The creativity, seriousness, and
intuitiveness of him stood out immediately. When he
chose movie roles, he made sure that it is different

from other movie roles. Also, he was sure to carry the spirit so that he played the roles genuinely. Despite the success on screen, he was using drugs, mouthing off at the media, and having health problems. His love life was unstable, as well. He had relationships with numerous actresses. Soon after, the turbulent relationship with the Australian press became more visible. The smiles and success couldn't hide it anymore. He was battling a respiratory illness. Things got so intense he took a heavy dose of pills. The amount made him feel energized, but it took his life as well. Through it all, he was smiling. I wish he moved forward amid the pain.

7. STANDARDS

Nia Long

*"Set High Standards, and Don't
be afraid to say no."*

You saw the beautiful Long in soap operas,
movies, and TV shows. Long was born in Brooklyn,
NY. She spent her childhood in Iowa and Los
Angeles. Moving forward was in her DNA. As she
grew, to do so became easier. She studied arts in
Iowa, and California was the last stop of her young
life. She graduated from St. Mary's Academy in
Inglewood, California. While in school, she studied
ballet, tap, jazz, gymnastics, guitar, and acting. A
woman with many avenues to success, but she chose
the road that leads to acting. After a while, she
became a leader on the screen. Despite being that, it
was still early, so she kept moving forward.
Eventually, an acting coach noticed her. That coach
starred in a show of her own, Betty Bridges, Different
Strokes. The main star on the show was actor Todd
Bridges. Her training sparked her to audition for one
of the most prominent roles in her career, and she

17

nailed it. After the audition, she'd get the part she desired. That role played the most prominent role in her career. She said, "It was a way to introduce me to the world. It told me that it is ok to be who I am and still find success. I still watch that movie after all of these years. Undoubtedly one of my favorite hood movies. The moral here is simple. Moving forward will bring attention. After a while, people will come to you. That is what all leaders do. I believe she had discouraging times. I believe she thought no one paid attention. Possibly, she shook off those times and moved forward and looked back. Like any leader, she was always ready.

8. PREPARED

Emma Watson

"It's not the absence of fear. It's overcoming it".

On my old Facebook account, I talked about this often. So, I started a new one. No longer could I access my business pages, my connections, and I cannot reset my code or anything. The hackers got into it and changed my email. Despite the unfortunate events, I always remember this quote by actress Emma Watson. A quote that encourages me always to be not shocked when it comes. The selection is, "It's Not the absence of fear. It's overcoming it". She's not the only one that said that. It always is there on the path to greatness. Our jobs are to overcome it. The spirit of fear was still present when I grew up. I was blind to it for 36 years of my life. On my last job, I fell sick five years ago. After recovering, there was a shift in my thinking. My eyes started seeing things differently, and my mind thought differently. To add to it, I faced my fears and drove my car to Atlanta, GA. The time came for me to face my fears and invest in the future. All leaders have to take these steps. Anxiety is on the pathway that leads to what we need. Our jobs are not complaining about it. Our jobs are to overcome it. So, we must be ready at all times. If you see fear, keep moving and applaud yourself for each step you take.

9. APPLAUD

Denzel Washington

"If You Don't Fail, you are not even trying."

When a baby is learning to walk, they fall. During it, the parents are sometimes applauding, yelling YOU GOT IT. I disregarded this scenario when I was younger. That was until a few years ago. Falling, I always hated, so I never moved, but the truth is, it's a part of life. A mindset shift opened my eyes and minded more to see that it happens. That baby eventually learned how to walk. Actor Denzel Washington said, "If you do not fail, you are not even trying." That was one of the quotes that made me look at things differently. No one wants to fall when they lead, but it happens when we're moving forward, and like those parents applaud their child, we should commend ourselves. We get back up, own up to it, and try again. Denzel Washington often played roles displaying the character of a leader doing just that. In the movie, HE GOT GAME; he owned up to his mistake. Throughout the film, he rekindled a broken relationship with his son. In the end, his son made the most critical decision of his life. Similar roles came to him along the way. Washington was more than an actor in these films. He was a leader that many young men need. Like this next actor, he made it count.

10. SERIOUS

Actor Alex O'Loughlin

"Make it Count."

Not his exact words, but I see what he meant. The new Hawaii 5-0 star is very adamant about this. I could admit that this is something I did not take seriously early on. My scenario to be an author I will use here. I write on numerous platforms. There were many ideas that I started in the past that have laid dormant for sometimes. To make a long story short, I was always active on social media sites. When Myspace and Black Planet were popular, I was there. In the last 10-15 years, it was Facebook, where I engaged in conversations that hurt me and did not make it count. Me hurting myself never crossed my mind until now. The moral is all in what made it count in a way that will not benefit me. Now, it's one of my biggest regrets. I try not to even think about it. I now have the mindset to make every opportunity count. As leaders, opportunities come to us. Either they go, or we find them. Frequently, I am online every day as I work from home. I see different options all of the time. Growing into leadership, you must learn to make everything count. By making it matter, I mean to take it seriously. Also, make sure that people are affected. In the end, you will not regret it. Believe in yourself, and it will happen but be humble too.

11. HUMBLE

Whitney Houston

"If You Believe."

I look for leadership in anything and anyone that I can, as you could see. I grew up believing I could do anything. I got older and had the same mentality. When I was young, I was pretty good at basketball. I had the dribbles and everything. At least I thought it. That led me to believe I could play for one of the top coaches in the community center near my complex. I went out for his team didn't make it. I took it as rejection. I tried out for another, and the reaction was different. I made the team, but that was a mistake. One that it took me years to see. That coach that rejected me saved me. My belief was there, but it was not enough. The late Whitney Houston echoed how important it is to believe in a song. She didn't inform many that it's not enough. She became that leading lady in the industry. It was evident early. She grew up around it all. So she knew what to do to be a part of it. Once in, she quickly rose to the top, just like she believed. The success came but so did what she thought wasn't. After years of it, she succumbed to it. Houston committed suicide, proving that belief is not enough. Confidence is reasonable, but it means nothing without humility. Rejection has saved many lives. Along with them, both have an environment to help you.

12. CREATORS

Sophia Turner

*"I think that you form the way
that you act from others around
you; it's kind of an environmental
thing."*

The key words I see here is form. Another name
for this is creating. When I was young, I often did
this. Growing up where I did, I had to. The
environment was accepted and loved, but it wasn't
non-toxic. My siblings and I had to develop this
quality of leadership. Sadly, we had no clue what we
created. When we joined a church, a member said we
don't know what we have very often. My siblings
possess these same qualities. Actress Sophia Turner
said, "I think you form the way you act from others
around you; it's kind of an environmental thing"
Now, this young actress understands leadership. She
was born in England to pretty successful parents.
Before she was born, she had a twin sister.
Unfortunately, at birth, the twin died. It was just her
and her two older brothers having fun in their

childhood home. During her childhood, she decided to pursue a career in drama. Her job became a success, but her focus was on creating the environment to stay that way. She succeeded in doing that too. That environment includes people. We need to be around people that will lift us. We create the ground, but it consisted of the wrong people. After many years we saw, and both learned, that we must create an environment with the right people. The right people and background will help it to remain productive. This next artist proved that we all fly, but sometimes, it's just in a cage.

13. FLY HIGH

Robert Kelly

"I believe I could fly."

He wrote it and much more. We all know him as a singer, songwriter, and producer R. Kelly. He is undoubtedly one of the best of all time. That song is one of the most inspirational pieces of my childhood. When I was a kid, I sometimes walked around with a towel tied to my shirt. I used to tuck it in my shirt and walk around like I'm DC's Superman. Many kids in the community did the same thing. We all felt like we could fly like our favorite heroes. That song is too on the soundtrack of one of the most iconic basketball films ever. The pain that he experienced as a child paved the way for that song and much more. He grew up and started flying. The piece revealed his belief, but it also revealed his struggles. Many say that he wrote it for mom that passed away, but I think there was a more significant reason. It was like a bird singing in a cage that was trying to get out. He was soaring, but it was inside a cell. He was an industry leader flying high, but he did not realize it. Outside of

29

Kelly, we do that too. We pass but are inside one area. We have to put our leadership into action.

14. ACTIONS

Mark Wahlberg

"Want and acting are two
different things."

Growing up in Boston, Massachusetts, I could imagine how wild things were there. His parents divorced when he was eleven years old. Things were made worse in his teenage years. At 13, he developed an addiction to crack cocaine and other substance abuse. By 16, he was into gangs and violence. His behavior was very aggressive. He often violated the civil rights of victims. The fact that his father was not in the household plays a considerable role. He took the first step to change and turned to a priest to help him turn from crime, and his street friends hated it. He became a teen idol on the stage as rapper Marky Mark. He was also into modeling and acting. Despite him turning away, he had consequences he had to go through. He was aware of the rough road ahead of him, but it would have been severe if he stayed into it. As a leader, he knew the right thing but struggled actually to do it. After years, he stopped working. By

2017, he topped the list of the world's highest-paid actors. He was so big; he even donated the funds he generated. He stared adversity in the face and overcame it. Leaders know how important it is not just to talk good but to act. They also take pride in being authentic.

15. AUTHENTIC

Janet Jackson

*"You don't have to hold on to
the pain to hold on to the memory,"*

I remember watching her on the show Good
Times. I grew up in an era when she and her brothers
were popular on the music scene. Not in the '70s but
the '90s. That show was not in the generation I grew
up in, but I love it. I still watch it when it comes on
now. Despite having such an entertaining family, her
inspiration wasn't them. She has spoken that
numerous singers opened doors, and she was one of
the artists that walked in it. Once in, she often was
noticed as the little sister. So much until she
requested, they did not mention it. She wanted to be
known for being who she is in her light. Janet felt
similar, but her brother was an icon. She fought hard
for the world to see her as her person. Now, she
doesn't even request it. They knew not to do it. She
portrayed the little girl's image they wanted her to,
but she was not happy. Janet wanted to be who she
was and forget the past. Being authentic is one

essential quality of leadership. We have to be pleased with who we are—being authentic. It is a must for us. The more precise we are, the more heroic we look.

16. HEROIC

Gal Gadot

"Be Persistent and never Give up."

She was born in 1985 in Israel. Her childhood was in a home not too far from where she was born. She possessed superhero qualities when she was young. She did two years in the Israeli Defense force as a combat instructor, and movie directors and producers noticed her unique quality. When she auditioned to play the role of Giselle in the movie franchise Fast N Furious, and she nailed it. Her next role defined who she was. She played wonder woman. The film told her life story. Her training included her being a warrior since she was little. In the movie, her mother tried to shield her from troubles. That's what mothers do. Mines still did that to me before I was stable. No matter how grown-up we are, a mother will always be one. I'm stable, so she doesn't worry. Let's get back to the film. In it, she earned her mother's trust. As leaders do, she showed she could hold her own. She battled as she faced a historical villain. The villain escaped from incarceration and threatened her homeland. In the end, she defeated him too. Before her own, the other film she appeared in was DC's movie Justice League. Her character inspired little girls worldwide to be heroic. Heroic but misunderstood at times.

17. MISJUDGED

Michael Jackson

"Believe in Yourself No Matter What"

The king of pop knew this, but he also knew how much he missed as a kid. I want to discuss how I think he felt. Jackson and his brothers were teen idols. Their success led to him being a well-established solo act, known for his leadership on the stage and off. Kids loved him, and he loved them. In 1982, he wrote and sung a song for the movie E. T the Extra-Terrestrial. For the song, he won Grammy for Best recording for children. As time went on, his love for children grew. He remembered his childhood. He wanted to do for kids what he never got for himself since he started performing at an early age. Over time, he built an empire, and it allowed him to make a theme park called Never Land in California. Despite his good intentions, some accused him of getting to close. His love for kids came with much confusion. 1993 was one of many accusations of child abuse he faced. From that time, he struggled with it.

His health started to fail—pills for pain and anything that gave him a sense of pleasure. Soon after, they raided his home. There was an out-of-court settlement in which he admitted to no wrongdoing and no liability. Jackson was free until he was charged for child abuse again a decade later. After a long battle, he succumbed to it. Sadly, this is an unfortunate aspect of leadership. Our aggression and passion not many understand. We take pride in having strength. Strength so that we could fight through Adversity.

18. WISDOM

Sylvester Stallone

"Big arms move rocks, but big words could move mountains."

That quote explained how it is vital to feed your mind. When your mind is fed right, you will be wise during trials & my trials, and tribulations. I remember this story. Stallone was born slightly paralyzed. He suffered from a stuttering problem, but his mind was healthy. Stallone was gifted to act and wanted to use it. He went to acting school and learned the craft. His determination made him a hit onboard. Shortly after, he was on the small and big screen. Writing and acting. One of his most iconic films, Rocky, was his rise to fame. There were roadblocks in his way. Blocks that made him settle for things that he now regrets in this present day. He and a friend wrote the screenplay for the film Rocky after seeing a Muhammad Ali fight. In just three days, they completed it. The success of the film led to some controversy. That friend sued him, but he and Stallone settled it. He was offered $350,000 for the rights to the film. He got more when he was the star. After that, he wrote more film scripts. Stallone was also writing novels, and Rambo was one of them. Despite no success, it was clear that he was one overseas and in America, but he felt otherwise. As a response, there was much heartache that led him to battles. Battles that he conquered. Now, he's the leader that he knew he would be.

19. LIFESTYLE

Lana Michelle Moore

"Make Goals for yourself and stop at nothing until you make it happen"

You know rapper MC Lyte? That's her real name. She was born and raised in New York. Her mom was a great example of a leader, and she wanted her daughter to do the same. So, her childhood was very strict. Safety was not an issue, nor was education— her mother led by example, significant. Also, the young Mc did not put limits on her life. People often speculated about her father's role in her young life, but it was just speculation. Nothing was proven to be true. While learning to lead by example, she fell in love with art. At age twelve, she was rapping and led by example ever since. To make matters better, she gained notoriety. Her successful career in hip hop came to an end. When the time came to step off the stage, she displayed more leadership. She became known as a businesswoman and designed a company that provides the leadership that young artists need.

She touched with music, and she's doing it without it. She led by example from the start. She was proving that it's a lifestyle all along. It's many avenues, but leadership is on them all.

20. GROW

Amy Smart

*" I think it is about growth. You
continue to grow and progress,
hopefully".*

Smart was in L.A, California. Her mom was a
museum worker, and her dad was a salesman. During
her childhood, she did not have to worry about much
about anything. For ten years, the young smart
showed that she would be the leader that she is today.
During those years, she studied ballet. Once she
graduated from high school, she started modeling.
She flew to Italy to pursue her dream, but she fell in
love with another while there. She began taking
lessons in acting. What stood out about her rise to
fame was the fact that she put herself in different
positions. She liked modeling and wanted it to be a
skill. So, she went to a modeling capital. Italy is
known for its models. While there for modeling, she
befriended model another female model that
introduced her to acting. They both found love for the
small and silver screen. Together they took acting

lessons when they flew back to Los Angeles. There are multiple streams, but it seemed that she chose the best one for her. Now, she's one of the female leaders on the big and small screen. Smart put herself in positions that will generate growth. That's what leaders do well. We lead on every avenue of this journey. Along the way, we valued our dignity.

21. DIGNITY

Michael B Jordan

*'Don't try to pretend to know
everything. Just be the best at it."*

He was born in Santa Ana, California. This actor I grew to love when I watched the movie, Black Panther. After that film, I started studying him in different films before it. Jordan's role in the film is Kill Munger. Munger is the estranged cousin of the superhero black panther. He saw his dead father as a child and wanted revenge. His uncle murdered his brother. The role he played was so good he admitted that it took a lot out of him. Simply I think that he thinks it wasn't him. He offered more and wanted to show that he can. Jordan wanted more of a part reflecting who he was. So, he acted as a lawyer fighting for an inmate to be free. Being a leader in the world of entertainment is hard. It's hard outside it so that I could imagine. They play roles that could degrade you. Numerous actors/actresses had a hard time with this very thing. They play their parts so well familiar people forget that it's just an act. Some spend much time convincing folk that it is an act. Different actors have turned down roles since they want to be in a different light. I admired that quote since it showed that he valued the dignity of his image. He values integrity as well, but this next actor does too.

22. INTEGRITY

James Franco

*"Create your world around your
work. Create your work around
your life. Let the other people help
you shape it."*

This actor has made it clear that he values
integrity. Since I knew of him, it's all he did. He was
born in 1978 in Palo Alto, California. His parents
gave him a somewhat averaged lifestyle. His
upbringing was academic, liberal, & mostly secular.
He was often encouraged to do well in school, and he
did, but he did wrong in the midst as well. He
struggled to value integrity when he was young.
Unfortunately, events include an arrested for
underage drinking, graffiti, and being part of a group
of thieves. None of those things stopped him from
graduating from High School in 1996. Seemingly, he
quickly started understanding it. Soon after, he
enrolled in the University of California and became
an English major. Secretly, he was studying theater
studies. It was sudden and a heartbreaker for his

parents when he dropped out and decided to pursue a career in acting. I could imagine how his parents felt; they were no longer supporting him. Despite the lack of support from parents, someone did help him become the actor he is today. Franco worked for it legally and studied his craft. For fifteen years, he trained to be who he is. The help needed found him. The value of integrity he finally understood. This next actress wasn't as lucky at first. Things were a bit different with this next actress. She was just resilient from the start.

23. RESILIENCE

Gabrielle Union

"Be Resilient"

Leaders know they make mistakes, and she is one of them that did. I could admit that she and her husband are not huge fans of the way I used to be. Nevertheless, I admire the leadership of the actress. Union was born in Omaha, Nebraska. As a child, she learned to be resilient. Her mother often provided adequate oversight during her childhood, but an event that took place not too far from almost took it all away for me. Union faced many unfortunate experiences in her early childhood. She grew up with self-esteem issues. In 1991, she was attacked and raped at a part-time job in a shoe store. Those events did not stop her from graduating from High School and college. Union had resilience as a child and a young adult. Thinking like a winner and became one was not hard for her. Now, she has a bachelor's degree in sociology. Her resilience was at an all-time high, but her childhood events took a toll on her attitude. A good friend of hers reminded her of that when they went to a party together. From that moment, Gabrielle made changes. She studied and became an actress, which revealed it all. Now she is wealthy and has an NBA ex-superstar alongside her. The two even had a child together. The moral to her story is right or wrong; leaders must be resilient. We must have no other desire but to win. We lose at times, but we carry that in our minds. Losing is an option, but we act like it is not. This next actress explains how adversity never leaves.

24. FEARLESS

Elizabeth Banks

"I am not afraid of much"

In Pittsfield, Massachusetts, Elizabeth Banks was born. As a child, she grew up catholic and very active. The young banks had no clue what adversity was until her health crises. Once she healed up, she tried out for the school play. Acting, she fell in love with immediately, and After graduating in 1992, she went to study it. She was well on her way, but Adversity was in the path. She joined The Junior Classical League, Delta Delta Delta, and the Fiers Senior Society at the University of Pennsylvania. Four years later, she had a degree in communications and a minor in theater arts. Two years later, she completed schooling at the American Conservatory Theater in San Francisco, California. She started adversity in the face and kept going. Now she's reached the goal she intended. What I like about what Banks did is how she just went for what she wanted. She saw the fear but remained focused. There is no shame in me saying that I struggled with that many times. When I saw fear, I felt it was easier to quit. Now, I never make excuses. As leaders, we must know that worry never leaves. This next musician shows the first thing needed if you want to overcome it. Facing them is how we build character.

25. CHARACTER

Stevie Wonder

"Ability will get you to the top,
but character helps you stay there".

He was born in Saginaw, Michigan in 1950. Out of six siblings, he is the third oldest. Obstacles were waiting for him as soon as he was born. One of them was a condition that made him blind. Additionally, family life was a bit unstable. Despite it all, he found his way to rise above it. Music was used as a way to escape. One of the active activities included singing in the church choir. In addition to him singing, he also started playing instruments. More activities included performing on the streets. Pretty soon, he captured the eyes of music executives. Soon he was another blind artist in the industry. They made no excuses and got there, and all had the character to remain there. Little boy Wonder became Stevie Wonder. I assume that his disability developed the consistency he needs. There was no struggle with having the character to stay on top. One with that mentality is undoubtedly a leader. Our unfortunate develops character the surface

53

to remain on top. At 70 years old, he has nine kids and a legacy in music that will never die. This actor often played the character the world needed and encouraged others along the way.

26. ENCOURAGE

Micheal Caine

" Even though I was poverty-stricken.I never thought I should give up".

I didn't become aware of this actor until the movie The Dark Knight. Michael Caine played the role so well; I started conducting more research. London is where he was born and raised. Additionally, it is where he faced many circumstances that made him develop the character. Acting became a considerable part of his success. On-screen, to help others create the feeling that he did. At just ten, he played in school plays. The role he played in one showed his maturity. Caine displayed great intellect at a very young age. As he grew, he got smarter and desired to solve problems. So, he joined the British military to do so in 1954. As anyone in the military, you are always at risk of losing your life. Truthfully, that's a risk every day. Caine experienced that, and it built the character he has today. His breakthrough 1960s and nothing's changed since then. My two surgeries before 35 years old is an example. All of those things I went through were building the character I needed in me. That's how leaders look at the unfortunate things that happen to us. Now, we intend to encourage others to build theirs. We recognize others need a push to lead, so we push the maximum level of encouragement.

27. MAXIMUM

Sade

*"Move in a Space with
Minimum waste and maximum
joy."*

This Nigerian born queen made leadership the
fashion statement that it is. Her childhood started in
England. At birth in 1959, she was named Helen Adu.
She found interest in fashion designing early. She
made it through school, and her interest grew. When
she graduated, she moved to London to pursue a
career in fashion design. She studied design and
started modeling. In three years, she finished a course
in fashion design. It wasn't long after when she fell
for music. A British band needed a backup singer.
She auditioned and got the part. This role led to a
partnership with one of the band members. After a
few gigs and a band breakup, she became famous—
Popular in London and the United States. As time
went on, she became a global sensation. What I like
about Sade was how she refused to settle. She went
for the max. Now at 61 years old, she has left her

mark. Us going for the maximum is common. Many of us do not settle in our DNA to always go for the max, so we will not be followers all of our lives.

28. UNFOLLOWS

Eddie Murphy

"Do not Follow the Crowd.

Murphy was born in Brooklyn, NY. He did not know anything about his father beside his charm. His father left his mother when he was three and died when he was eight. At that same age, his mother became ill. Murphy would then live in foster care for a year until his mother recovered. Murphy's' journey to comedy started at 15. He was so successful as a comedian; he got the attention of executives. They offered him a job to be a part of one of the most successful late-night programs on T.V. SATURDAY NIGHT LIVE. The show was suffering hard times in the '80s. Murphy revived it after the five years of low ratings. After success on T.V, he moved to the big screen. His first film was in 1982 (48 hrs.). In 1983, he starred in the movie TRADING PLACES. Each year, he was in a movie. In 1988, he starred as a prince visiting the United States. The movie is COMING TO AMERICA. Now, the movie is still iconic. The success of the film was huge at the box office, but the controversy was too. As time went on, he was nominated and won awards. Murphy was himself since he started his career; he never really followed the crowd. That is a typical feature of a leader. Now him being himself did come with controversy. Murphy hurt people following the group. Now he leads them. Those he followed were not the support systems he needed.

29. SYSTEM

Jim Carrey

"Depression is your mind telling you that it is tired of being the character that you're trying to play."

Wow, I never thought of it that way. That quote is better than his one about systems. Funnyman Jim Carrey made a quote about support systems. He was born In a small town in Toronto, Canada; he was born. His mom was a homemaker, and his father was a musician/accountant. His religious background is roman catholic. During that time, his family struggles were pretty high. Despite the efforts, he laughed his way through it. When he was just ten years old, he was already a master of impressions. He became funnier as he grew up, but his family struggles grew too. In the midst of it all, he still had their support. Things were so intense he dropped out of school. Dropped out and started performing at comedy nightclubs. Soon the struggles became nearly monumental. They only did what they could. After a while, the finances were not there. That alone discouraged him, but he did not stop. His family all stretched out and worked hard. He struggled to make a name for himself. Of course, he struggled with his beliefs at this point. He got himself together and tried it again. Soon after, he struck gold. He realized that he always had a system that always supported him. His family never allowed him to fold. This next pioneer grew up in times when folk saw blacks as rejects. She let it move her instead of being complacent.

30. PEACE OF MIND

Cicely Tyson

*"Money is not important to me,
but Peace of mind is."*

Tyson was born In 1924. She is now labeled one of the pioneers on the silver screen. That's good, but I think she does not get enough credit as a one-off of it. Her mother is named Fredrica, and her father is named William. Tyson started in fashion. Before the big screen, she was a model. Over time, much popularity came her way. Since she was good at modeling, why not? But she wanted to act. In 1951, she got her chance. Her role in the series Frontiers of Faith, she blazed a trail. On the stage, T.V, and the movie screen success spanned over decades. Over those decades, she earned the right to be called a pioneer in the entertainment world. One of the reasons I feel she is not given credit off of the screen enough is due to her leadership. She made a leadership quote about rejection and having peace of mind. A sacrifice moved her to have peace of mind. In her early years, I could imagine the rejection she faced. The fact that she allowed it to drive her to be the pioneer that she amazes me. Tyson's actions surprised me, along with leaders around the world. Since of her, I know that hard work hard pays off. Along with working hard, they had to use rejection to move and motivate them at all times.

31. MOTIVATED

Forest Whitaker

*"You have to give respect to get
it back."*

A simple quote said by a simple man. He was
born in Texas in 1961. His childhood was split there
and in California. He is the youngest of four. The
acting was always there since he in his DNA waiting
to be activated. He just did not know it early on. He
engaged in numerous activities in high school. One of
them was football. He got an athletic scholarship to
play at California State Polytechnic University. After
a fatal incident, he had ended it and changed his
major. He changed his major to music since singing
was an option. The choir he was in at his school was
on tour. England was one of the stops. At the same
time, what was in his DNA activated. He returned and
was more motivated. Now At age 59, Whitaker built
himself an established legacy. He has a long history
of working with producers and directors. In his first
acting role on the big screen, he played the role of a
football player. After that film, His career took off. I

loved the way he acted in films Jason's Lyric, Taken 3. and Black Panther. Now, he is producing and directing himself. What I love about Whitaker's' story is how he stayed motivated. He remained motivated and directly has inspired someone else.

32. INSPIRE

Jennifer Hudson

"Do not block your blessings.
Do not let doubt stop you from
getting where you need to be. "

Wonderfully said from the Chicago native. She is not only a songbird; she is an actress. Before she was ten years old, Hudson was singing in choirs with her voice. Like her grandmother inspired her, she wanted to inspire others. After graduating from high school, pursuing her dream was her desire. American Idol was in town, and she auditioned. That show introduced her to the world. Despite a loss, her career took off on the stage. She also acted and inspired many just with her voice. There were also issues, and one of them was her weight. She wasn't though to make it, and her image may have played a role. Now expectations are exceeded. She lost weight and made it no longer an issue. By now, she may have lost more than that. On a talk show, she said, "I don't have time to work out, so I watch what I eat, and I eat in portions. I watch what I put in my body." That is what amazed me the most about her story. Not only did she not doubt herself, but she also maintained her body. Now, she is inspiring others to change and have order in their lives.

33. ORDER

Sandra Bullock

" You must have Order In Your Life."

She never had an issue with order growing up. She was born in Arlington, Virginia, in 1964. Her father was an Army commander, and her mom was an opera singer. Much of her childhood was in Germany and Austria. I started studying the actress's story after I saw her in the movie Speed. As I looked at her lifestyle, I noticed that she's a German citizen and an American. She spent her childhood in different places, but there was order wherever she was. She started studying acting in 1982. As her love for it grew, she moved to the city where many have started, New York City. The chances there were fantastic, and she took off. This actress displayed much on and off the screen. Her orderly ways are often on display. Her image in the media was often friendly. As I studied her posture in films, I could see it. Since I started seeing things differently, I see something I usually do not see. When she said a quote about it, it was just confirmation. As leaders, it is a mandate that we have the order. The ruling makes it easier to walk in truth.

34. TRUTH

Idris Elba

"Walk in Truth."

He was born in London in 1972. Elba's first name at birth was a bit difficult to announce. Besides that, I don't think that he liked it very much. So, he decided to shorten it to Idris. He fell in love with acting, but his passion for hip hop was in the way when he chose to pursue it. He became a rapper and started his own DJ company. Before being known as a rapper, he was a DJ. He was DJ at events all around London. He also did show when asked—rapping paved the way for his acting career. All the while, he was auditioning for roles. He remained true to his first love acting. So, walking into doing it was not hard. Once he made enough, he went forth. He played small roles around London. Those roles helped him get on a bigger platform. Prominent movie executives and producers took notice around the globe. Now, he is the actor of many talents. He remained loyal to acting. Even when other skills came along the way for

Elba, he stayed right to it and aimed to perfect it. He knew the value of time and that it waits for no one.

35. TIME

Robert Deniro

"Whatever you need to do, do it now." Simple, demanding, and very clear, He said that "

Time Goes On and not to wait. He was born in Manhattan, NY. He grew up in a small town called Little Italy. The zeal to act came to him early. At age ten, he was the cowardly lion in the stage play, The Wizard of Oz, at his school. As time grew, his love for the stage did. He found performing as a way to help him defeat his timidness. It was not long when he fell in love with the cinema. At just sixteen, he dropped out of high school and chose to pursue acting. Dropping out of school is often against wishes. He is one of the many celebrity actors that chose this path to start things out. De Niro is now 77. His quote is proof that he stood by that. I would not have done something that way, but I see why he and many actors did. Time waits for no man. That quote reminds me of another quote that said, "It does not have to be right to get it going." If you know the right thing, do it. Time is not going to wait for you. Most leaders stand by that. We think fast as we lead. We all have a mindset to overcome since we know that the clock is ticking.

36. OVERCOME

Sherri Shepard

*"If you do not go towards the
thing you fear, you won't be able to
say that you lived. "*

Being born and raised in Chicago, she had to face
hers to be who she is now. Her parents are named
LaVerne and Lawrence D. Shepherd. She and her
sisters grew up in a religious setting. With that
setting, they often overcame much that came their
way. She did it and became an actress, but her
problems didn't end. In the early stages, she lost
much. She lost her apartment, her car, her dignity,
and she slept on other people's couches. Despite it all,
she remained focused and overcame it. She said that
in the business of acting, it is uncertain. You could be
working one day and not the next. I could add to that
and say Nothing in Life Is. So, overcoming needs to
be flowing throw our veins. There is always
something going to be in the way that we must
overcome. Her story alone proves that there is still
something. When you are a leader, you have to

overcome as you go on. I tell anyone there are struggles in everything you do. A mindset to overcome is what I obtained, and most leaders I know. Overcoming is easy when you do not let the struggles get to you.

37. UNASHAMED

Emily Blunt

*"It is nothing to be ashamed of
to have a stutter."*

I assume she was talking about her problem. She
was born and raised in London. Her childhood home
was not too far from her birthplace. There were
difficulties she faced during her childhood and teen
years. She had a severe stuttering problem, but it was
not severe enough to stop her from pursuing acting.
At age sixteen, she went to school for it, then an agent
discovered her. By 2001 she was ready to make her
professional debut as an actress. A few years later,
she got her breakthrough. That severe stuttering
problem was non-existent at this point. Now, she is a
wife, a mother, is a dual citizen of the United States.
Like all of us, I am sure she saw struggles. They are
on every leader's path, and our job is not to let them
beat us. Beat them and show people that the real
monster is not you.

38. GOOD GUYS

Shemar Moore

"Acting is Therapeutic."

Most things are that people are passionate about are. I often tell people to do what you love. Thus, That is an excellent quote by the actor, but I want to talk about one that he said when he was acting. His skills to perform came to him when he was a child. As a child, he values education was prominent. Moore was placed in British Private School when he was seven. When he got older and graduated high school, he fell in love with Theater. Acting is one of those childhood skills. For eight years, he acted on the hit soap opera The Young and Restless. He also is a host and a model. I remember a quote from one of the episodes of Criminal Minds. "Yes, there are monsters, and it's OK to be afraid of them. It's not okay to let them win, and it's not ok to be one". That is a leadership quote. We are aggressive, demanding, but we are the good guys. Our destiny is to be heroes in their stories and our own.

39. ROLE MODELS

Gerard Butler

"Be a Hero in Your Story."

The Scotland native did not need many words to get his point across here. He is the youngest of three children by Margaret and Edward Butler. As an infant, he moved to Canada. School activities kept him out of trouble during his teen years. Like any other kid that's a boy, he missed his dad. When his dad resurfaced, he was still upset. By this time, he decided to act. Along his young journey, he studied law and sang in a rock band. Things were going well until his father died when he was 22 years old. He became out of control, but he regained it. The road to being an actor started in London. It was rocky when it began, but his desire to began an example would not let him quit. He befriended a casting director and became her assistant. That was just the position he needed. He was catapulted into the position to act. At age 27, Butler had his first professional acting job. He moved to the U.S, and things got better. That hero became a reality. He also became that example. The desire to be examples drives us. So along the way, we find hope.

40. HOPE

Danny Glover

"Find Hope In Your Struggles."

He did just that when he was a kid. He was born and raised in San Francisco, California. His childhood was pretty orderly. During it, he was diagnosed with epilepsy. So he had no choice but to find hope. He suffered to 35 but has had none since. That's what hope will do. His story relates to me. I am on epilepsy medication. I had a mild seizure on my job. I had to find hope all through it. When I am stressed out, it is easier for them to come. I took the 500 milligrams of Keppra two times a day for multiple years. I remember when I had one. I moved to Atlanta, GA, and had another mod one at the age of 36. I was working too hard, which triggered it. After a few hours in the hrs in the hospital, I was ok. Through it all, I still had hope. That hope that Danny Glover has right now. It was not easy to find it as I was in that situation, but I did. I ignored the circumstance. Having hope is what any leader should have. We need it as we lead to remain strong despite the chaos around me.

41. CHAOS

Ryan Reynolds

"Chaos Drives Us."

This topic, I think it's the most sensitive to us all. Chaos comes to us all. Some have let it control them. I could admit that I did for 34 years of my life, but now, I allow it to push me. Reynolds comes from a family of police officers. He never took acting classes to do what he loved. He just knew the skill. Thinking this way about chaos is Unique and enjoyable. With this, you must be careful, so you do not miss it. Reynolds was born and raised in Canada. He is the youngest of four brothers. Reynolds seemed to have developed a niche to act, so he studied it. His career started in 1991. He has done shows in Canada, and a few years later, he was prominent in the U.S. What he said about chaos is what I want to explain here. Due to what he said about the mess, I assume that's what drove him to stardom. That's what goes us all. Knowing where it goes us Is up to us. In the midst of all of this chaos, our leaders stand tall.

42. STAND

Linnethia Monique

*"Stand for What you Believe
in."*

I wouldn't call her much of an actress, but she is undoubtedly a TV personality. She vowed not to return to the shows that made many know who she is. I assume that she desires to be in a different light. Many know her as Nene Leakes. She was born in Queens, NY, but her childhood was spent in Athens, GA. As I studied her, there were some shows during my childhood that featured her. After my graduation, I found out that she played small roles in the background. I thought the Real Housewives of Atlanta was the place it all began. It turns out; it was her breakthrough. On the show, it's evident that she had no problems standing up for anything. Significantly when she believed in it all of my life, I did this. I always stood up for what I believed in, even if it was wrong. I did not realize that it was a vital aspect of a leader. At 30 years old, I found that it was. Now when I stand up, I am valuing honesty as well.

43. HONESTY

Minka Kelly

"I think brutal honesty is important,"

Her life started in L.A. Her father is a famous guitarist of a rock band who was not in her life. Her late mom raised her in many places before settling in New Mexico. Kelly was a junior in high school when she found out about tragic news. At age 51, her mother passed away from colon cancer. I assume that did take a toll since that was her mom. She may have found comfort in doing what she loved, and that was acting. Before it, she had an interest in modeling and being in the medical field. Despite her many talents, her first love was working. Now there are that do, but she wasn't going to ignore it. Being true to what you love makes life much more comfortable. Kelly is proof that valuing honesty will take you far. If you do not appreciate honesty, you may be doing the wrong thing. Right or wrong, you must love your work. Things are just better when it's right.

44. LOVE

Charles S Dutton

"Love Your Work,"

His acting proves that he does. He was born in 1951 in Baltimore, Maryland. Where he was born is not too far from where he grew up. He was often in trouble as a kid. One of those troubles were fighting. He dropped out of school before middle school to become an amateur boxer, but the stint was short-lived. Boxing was an attempt to stay out of trouble, but instead, there was more. At age 16, he was in a fight that resulted in death, and he was the suspect. The troubles lasted for some time and landed him behind bars. There, he fell in love with drama, and he wanted to start a drama program. Upon release, he returned to school and got his GED. A few years later, he completed a two-year college program for his degree in Associate of arts. Also, he earned a Bachelor of Arts in Drama and a Master's Degree in Acting. He loved the work when he was in jail and showed it outside it. Many leaders could relate here since we are all opportunists looking for opportunities like this.

45. OPPORTUNISTS

Chris Hemsworth

"Turn Opportunities into Something."

He sure turned his into something mighty. Most of his brothers are actors. His mom was a teacher, and dad was a social-services counselor. He's the middle child in the family. He grew up in Australia with his family. Since acting wasn't far from his lineage, it was not hard for him to fall into it. I think he inherited the skill when he was young. He first acted on T.V. on soap opera Home and Away, in Sydney, Australia. The soap opera gained him exposure but not the respect that he wanted. He still appreciated the opportunity. That exposure brought him more opportunities. After a while of direction, he got his breakthrough. I know him most as Thor in the trilogy. He played the same character in the Avengers movie franchise. From then, there were lightning bolts of opportunities. We are opportunists that look to invest. Some we take and some we despise. He saw any opportunity as exposure until he got his breakthrough. Now, he is shining in his light.

46. WISDOM

Tracee Ellis-Ross

*"Choose now what will make
sense later."*

I just found out a few years ago that she is the daughter of Motown legend Diana Ross. She looks just like her; the skin is slightly lighter. She was born in L. A but she was rarely there as a child. With an icon as a mom, I could imagine that she spent much of her childhood moving. She attended The Dalton School in Manhattan, NY. Riverdale Country School in the Bronx, NY, and Institute Le Roses in Switzerland. During the moving activity, she was modeling. In college, she started acting. She later obtained a degree in theater. I think she wanted her light. Being the child of a legend, you do not have too much to work for, but she felt she did. All that she did aim for what she desired. On her sitcom in the past, I had no clue who she was. When I found our I figured that she wanted her light and not her mom's. Her most recent film shows that she has a voice like her too. She never denounced it but wanted her light to

shine. We leaders want things to be the exact way.
Our light makes our personalities shine brightly.

47. SHINE

Natalie Portman

" Allow Your Personality to Shine. "

I think that this actress had a different purpose than on screen. She was born in Jerusalem to Jewish Parents. She and her family lived in Washington, Connecticut, and New York. I could imagine what she saw. She studied ballet and dance at the American Theater Dance Workshop. In the midst, she was around people that aimed to act. Her ambitious character separated her from the other kids when she was a child. She was severe then and grew up that way. She's studied multiple languages since she was ten years old. Her becoming a great actress was evident. Despite the facts spoken here, the opinion stated above stands.   I think she shines brighter as an activist. She fights for animal rights. At eight, she became a Vegan. In 2009, it was official. She despises wearing animal clothes and has given significant praise to animal lovers. Lastly, she is an advocate for the climate. She shines on-screen and off of it. The reflection helps us keep our vision clear.

48. CLEAR

Nasir bin Olu Dara Jones

"Keep your Vision clear"

Many know him as the New York rapper Nas. He was born on September 14, 1973, in Brooklyn, New York. His father was a musician from Mississippi who made sure to instill in him what he knew. He decided to walk in his father's steps when he was a kid. Growing up in New York made it more accessible. There, he found a great love in Hip Hop. Later, he became known as a rapper. On the streets, his nickname was Kid Wave. Since a child, he tried to keep his vision clear. I could imagine how hard it was growing up where he did. He saw his parents growing apart. In 1985, they made it official and divorced. That alone took a toll on the teen. He dropped out of school before he went to high school. Despite all of that, he kept feeding his brain. That's how he was able to see clearly. He grew to be the guy of many talents. When your vision is clear, you could see past the hurt around you. You could also see the energy that you spread.

49. CONTAGIOUS

Robert Van Winkle

"Spread Good Energy"

Some know him as a remodeler for homes, and others know him as the rapper Vanilla Ice. Ice had one of the big songs of my time. In 1967, he was born in Dallas, Texas, and his real dad was not there. So his mom's boyfriend took the mantle. Winkle took on the last name of his stepdad, whom he felt was his real one. He stayed in Texas and Miami. His energy was quite evident. You could tell that he was eager to share it. Van Winkle was into cycling, and he shined there. When he was not doing stunts, he was on the streets dancing. While in Miami, Vanilla Ice emerged. Before returning to Texas, he was a rapper. He dropped out of school and wrote his first rap song. His love for hip hop began to become noticed. On stage, he was named Vanilla Ice. Ice and his friends would perform around the city. The eyes and ears he caught were not just the cities. Big names came to him. Vanilla Ice's energy was contagious. Sadly, that career in music ended. Despite the end, he spread energy elsewhere. Now, he's selling and re-doing homes. We apply power but want it to be right. Since the energy we spread is contagious, it has no limits.

50. UNLIMITED

Lauryn Hill

*"There is always a chance to
make it right."*

I always thought that she was underrated. She was
born in New Jersey in 1975. Her parents were strict
about school. Maybe it"s since she is their only girl
too, so they want the best. She is also their youngest
child. She and her family spent little time in New
Jersey. They were very oriented when it came to
music. Her mom played the piano, and her father used
to sing. Her environment was music all of the time.
Growing up, she listened to Gladys Knight, Curtis
Mayfield, Stevie Wonder, and Aretha Franklin. When
she was young, she chose to walk in her father's
steps. After seeing him on stage, she loved it. Her
love grew, and her voice was beautiful. In middle
school, she sang before her school basketball game.
She had her chance to be recognized, and she was.
That recognition encouraged her to try out for the
SHOWTIME AT THE APOLLO, which shined a
light on her talent. She stood on that big stage in front
of hundreds. Sadly, her beautiful voice was not

attractive enough. She received a severe reaction from the crowd that led her to tears. Hill knew she could and desired not to let it limit her. After she cried, she stepped on a different stage in high school. She also became involved in other activities outside of music. The music always found its way to her. Hill not only was singing, but she was again rapping and acting as well. She faced all without limits. Those tears she shed at Apollo sparked more. Leaders are unlimited, and she proved it.

CONCLUSION

When I applied for this project, I had no clue what it was. When I was assigned to be apart of it, I was excited. I heard of it, and that grew too. As I mentioned here in the book, leadership, we are born with it. It's a lifestyle.
https://leademup.com/leadership-is-a-lifestyle/

All of these named here have qualities of a leader. I'm not a big fan of most, but I could give credit where it is due. Leadership is everywhere. Just open your mind to see it.
https://www.google.com/amp/s/simplifypersonalprod
uctivity.wordpress.com/2013/04/17/leaders-can-be-
found-anywhere-and-everywhere/amp/

The most important tip here is by actress/singer Lauryn Hill. There is no limit to leadership. We cry, hurt, and get stressed out like any human being, but we rise. There is no breaking point for us.
https://leadershipunlimited.org/

READ OTHER

50 THINGS TO KNOW

BOOKS

50 Things to Know

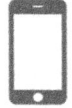

Stay up to date with new releases on Amazon:

https://amzn.to/2VPNGr7

50 Things to Know

Please leave your honest review of this book on Amazon and Goodreads. We appreciate your positive and constructive feedback. Thank you.